P9-CQG-399

SUPER SIMPLE

HEALTHY
cookies

EASY COOKIE RECIPES FOR KIDS!

ALEX KUSKOWSKI

Consulting Editor, Diane Craig, M.A./Reading Specialist

Super Sandcastle

An Imprint of Abdo Publishing
abdopublishing.com

abdopublishing.com

Published by Abdo Publishing, a division of ABDO, PO Box 398166, Minneapolis, Minnesota 55439. Copyright © 2016 by Abdo Consulting Group, Inc. International copyrights reserved in all countries. No part of this book may be reproduced in any form without written permission from the publisher. Super SandCastle™ is a trademark and logo of Abdo Publishing.

Printed in the United States of America, North Mankato, Minnesota
102015
012016

THIS BOOK CONTAINS RECYCLED MATERIALS

Editor: Liz Salzmann
Content Developer: Nancy Tuminelly
Cover and Interior Design and Production: Mighty Media, Inc.
Photo Credits: Mighty Media, Inc., Shutterstock

The following manufacturers/names appearing in this book are trademarks:
Arm & Hammer®, Brer Rabbit®, Calumet®, Krinos®, Market Pantry™, Philadelphia®, Proctor Silex®, Roundy's®

Library of Congress Cataloging-in-Publication Data
Kuskowski, Alex, author.
  Super simple healthy cookies : easy cookie recipes for kids! / Alex Kuskowski.
    pages cm. -- (Super simple cookies)
  ISBN 978-1-62403-948-5
1. Cookies--Juvenile literature. 2. Baking--Juvenile literature. I. Title.
  TX772.K776 2016
  641.86'54--dc23
                        2015020593

Super SandCastle™ books are created by a team of professional educators, reading specialists, and content developers around five essential components—phonemic awareness, phonics, vocabulary, text comprehension, and fluency—to assist young readers as they develop reading skills and strategies and increase their general knowledge. All books are written, reviewed, and leveled for guided reading and early reading intervention programs for use in shared, guided, and independent reading and writing activities to support a balanced approach to literacy instruction.

TO ADULT HELPERS

Help your child learn to cook! Cooking lets children practice math and science. It teaches kids about responsibility and boosts their confidence. Plus they get to make some great food!

Before getting started, set ground rules for using the kitchen, cooking tools, and ingredients. There should always be adult supervision when use of a sharp tool, oven, or stove is required. Be aware of the symbols below that indicate when special care is necessary.

So, put on your apron and get ready to cheer on your new chef!

SYMBOLS

Hot!
This recipe requires the use of a stove or oven. You will need adult supervision and assistance.

Sharp!
This recipe includes the use of a sharp utensil such as a knife or grater. Ask an adult to help out.

Nuts!
This recipe includes nuts. Find out whether anyone you are serving has a nut allergy.

CONTENTS

SWEET TREATS & HEALTHY EATS

Make sweet treats that are good for you too! Start baking healthy cookies. Healthy cookies have fruits and vegetables in the ingredients. They will fill you up without a lot of sugar. They make **delicious** snacks any time.

The healthy cookie **recipes** in this book are super simple. Cooking teaches you about food, measuring, and following directions. And you get to have delicious cookies! Share your tasty creations with family and friends.

 # COOKING BASICS

Think Safety!

- Ask an adult to help you use a knife. Place things on a cutting board to cut them.

- Clean up spills right away.

- Keep things away from the edge of the table or **counter**.

- Ask an adult to help you use the oven.

- Ask for help if you cannot reach something.

Using the Oven

- Preheat the oven while making the **recipe**.

- Use oven-safe dishes.

- Use pot holders or oven mitts to hold hot things.

- Do not touch the oven door. It can be very hot.

- Set a timer. Check the food and bake longer if needed.

Before Baking

- Get **permission** from an adult.

- Wash your hands.

- Read the recipe at least once.

- Set out the ingredients and tools you will need.

- Keep a **towel** close by for cleaning up spills.

When You're Done

- Let the cookies cool completely.

- Store the cookies in **containers**. Put a sheet of waxed paper in between the **layers** of cookies.

- Put all the ingredients and tools away.

- Wash all the dishes and **utensils**. Clean up your work space.

MEASURING INGREDIENTS

Wet Ingredients

Set a measuring cup on the **counter**. Add the liquid. Stop when it reaches the amount you need. Check the measurement from eye level.

Dry Ingredients

Dip the measuring cup or spoon into the dry ingredient. Fill it with a little more than you need. Use the back of a dinner knife to remove the extra.

Moist Ingredients

Measure ingredients such as brown sugar and dried fruit differently. Press them down into the measuring cup.

DID YOU KNOW THIS = THAT?

There are different ways to measure the same amount.

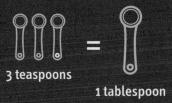 =
3 teaspoons ... **1 tablespoon**

4 tablespoons ... **¼ cup**

5 tablespoons + **1 teaspoon** = **⅓ cup**

 =
16 tablespoons ... **1 cup**

 =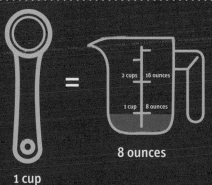
1 cup ... **8 ounces**

2 cups | 16 ounces
1 cup | 8 ounces

1 stick of butter ... **½ cup**

2 cups | 16 ounces
1 cup | 8 ounces
2 cups ... **1 pint**

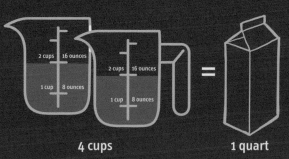
2 cups | 16 ounces
1 cup | 8 ounces
2 cups | 16 ounces
1 cup | 8 ounces
4 cups ... **1 quart**

2 quarts ... **½ gallon**

9

COOKING TERMS

CHOP

Chop means to cut into small pieces.

STIR

Stir means to mix ingredients together, usually with a spoon or rubber spatula.

SPREAD

Spread means to make a smooth **layer** with a spoon, knife, or rubber spatula.

WHISK

Whisk means to beat quickly by hand with a whisk or a fork.

KITCHEN UTENSILS

peeler

spatula

measuring spoons

measuring cups

electric mixer

cutting board

pot holders

blender

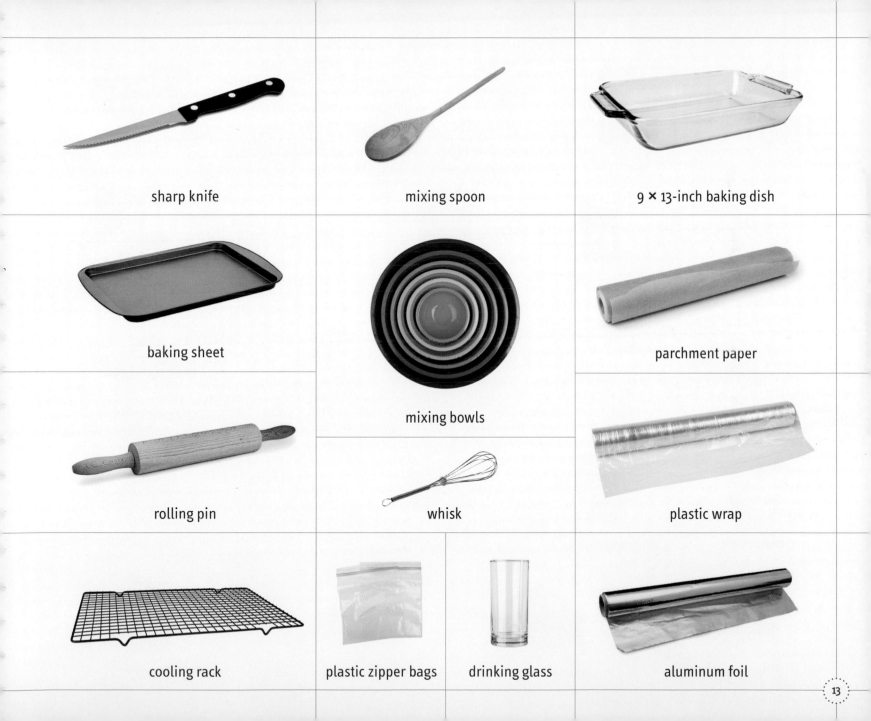

sharp knife

mixing spoon

9 × 13-inch baking dish

baking sheet

mixing bowls

parchment paper

rolling pin

whisk

plastic wrap

cooling rack

plastic zipper bags

drinking glass

aluminum foil

INGREDIENTS

all-purpose flour

almond flour

apples

applesauce

baking powder

baking soda

bananas

beets

brown sugar

butter

canola oil

cocoa powder

cream cheese

crunchy peanut butter

dried apricots

eggs

flaked coconut

flax seeds

ground cinnamon

ground ginger

honey

molasses

nutmeg

oat bran

oat flour

old-fashioned oats

olive oil

raisins

raspberries

raspberry jam

salt

sea salt

semi-sweet chocolate chips

sesame seeds

sliced almonds

sunflower seeds

tahini

vanilla extract

vanilla yogurt

walnuts

wheat germ

white sugar

whole wheat flour

15

chocolate surprise bites

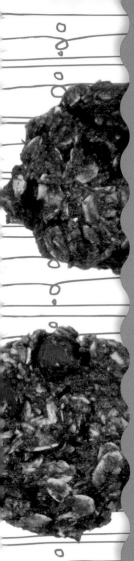

INGREDIENTS

2 tablespoons cocoa
powder

¾ cup old fashioned oats

6 tablespoons oat flour

¼ teaspoon salt

6 tablespoons white
sugar

¼ cup semi-sweet
chocolate chips

¼ cup applesauce

1 teaspoon vanilla extract

· · · · · · · · · · · · · · · · ·

TOOLS

mixing bowls

measuring cups

measuring spoons

rubber spatula

plastic zipper bag

large drinking glass

parchment paper

spoon

1. Put the cocoa powder, oats, oat flour, salt, sugar, and chocolate chips in a large bowl. Stir well.

2. Put the applesauce, vanilla, and 2 tablespoons water in a small bowl. Stir well.

3. Add the applesauce mixture to the oat mixture. Stir well.

4. Put the dough in a plastic bag. Refrigerate it for 30 minutes.

5. Roll the dough into 1-inch (2.5 cm) balls. Set them on parchment paper. Flatten them with a spoon.

gluten-free sesame

COOKIES

MAKES 15 cookies

INGREDIENTS

¼ cup sesame seeds

1¼ cups almond flour

¼ teaspoon salt

½ teaspoon baking soda

⅓ cup honey

⅓ cup tahini

1 tablespoon butter

1 tablespoon vanilla
extract

· · · · · · · · · · · · · · · · · ·

TOOLS

baking sheets

parchment paper

measuring cups

measuring spoons

mixing bowls

mixing spoon

electric mixer

drinking glass

pot holders

spatula

cooling rack

1 Preheat the oven to 350 degrees. Cover the baking sheets with parchment paper. Put the sesame seeds in a small bowl.

2 Stir the flour, salt, and baking soda together in a small bowl. Put the honey, tahini, butter, and vanilla in a large bowl. Mix with an electric mixer. Add the flour mixture to the honey mixture. Mix well.

3 Roll the dough into 1-inch (2.5 cm) balls. Coat each ball with sesame seeds. Put the balls on the baking sheet.

4 Flatten each ball with the bottom of a glass. Bake for 15 minutes. Put the cookies on a cooling rack.

sweet molasses

COOKIES

INGREDIENTS

2 cups whole wheat flour

1½ teaspoons baking soda

¼ teaspoon salt

1½ teaspoons ground cinnamon

1 teaspoon ground ginger

¾ cup molasses

½ cup brown sugar

¾ cup olive oil

1 egg

TOOLS

measuring cups

measuring spoons

mixing bowls

electric mixer

baking sheets

parchment paper

pot holders

spatula

cooling rack

1 Put the flour, baking soda, salt, cinnamon, and ginger in a medium bowl.

2 Put the molasses, brown sugar, oil, and egg in a large bowl. Mix with an electric mixer.

3 Add the flour mixture to the molasses mixture. Mix well. Refrigerate the dough for 1 hour.

4 Preheat the oven to 350 degrees. Cover the baking sheets with parchment paper.

5 With wet hands roll the dough into 1½-inch (3.8 cm) balls. Place each ball on the baking sheet.

6 Bake for 11 minutes. Put the cookies on a cooling rack.

nutty oat squares

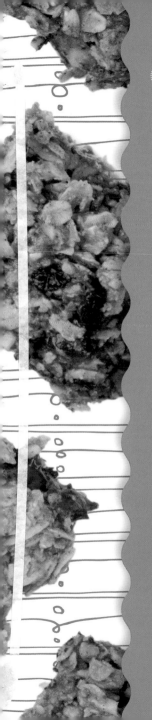

INGREDIENTS

3½ cups quick cooking oats

¾ cup raisins

⅔ cup sunflower seeds

½ cup sliced almonds

½ cup wheat germ

½ cup oat bran

3 tablespoons flax seeds

1 tablespoon ground cinnamon

1 teaspoon salt

1½ cups crunchy peanut butter

1 cup honey

¼ cup butter, melted

⅓ cup applesauce

½ cup semi-sweet chocolate chips

. . . .

TOOLS

9 × 13-inch baking dish

aluminum foil

measuring cups

measuring spoons

mixing bowls

mixing spoon

rubber spatula

pot holders

1. Preheat the oven to 350 degrees. Cover the baking dish with aluminum foil.

2. Put the oats, raisins, sunflower seeds, almonds, wheat germ, oat bran, flax seeds, cinnamon, and salt in a large bowl. Stir well.

3. Stir in the peanut butter, honey, butter, applesauce, and chocolate chips.

4. Press the mixture evenly into the baking dish.

5. Bake for 10 minutes. Take the baking dish out of the oven. Let it cool for 5 minutes.

giant breakfast
COOKIES

MAKES 12 LARGE COOKIES

INGReDIenTs

3 apples

3 cups whole wheat flour

3 cups old-fashioned oats

1⅓ cup brown sugar

1 tablespoon ground cinnamon

1½ teaspoons salt

1½ teaspoons baking soda

1 cup chopped walnuts

2¾ cups applesauce

½ cup canola oil

3 eggs

. . . .

TOOLS

baking sheets

parchment paper

peeler

sharp knife

cutting board

measuring cups

measuring spoons

mixing bowls

mixing spoon

whisk

pot holders

spatula

cooling rack

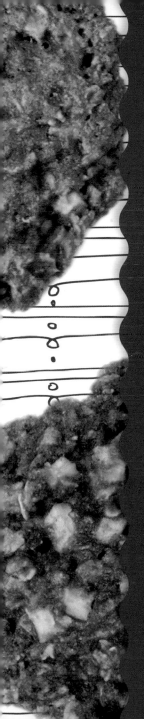

1   Preheat the oven to 350 degrees. Cover the baking sheets with parchment paper. Peel the apples. Cut them into small pieces.

2   Put the flour, oats, brown sugar, cinnamon, salt, baking soda, apples, and walnuts in a large bowl. Stir well.

3   Whisk the applesauce, oil, and eggs together in a medium bowl.

4   Add the applesauce mixture to the flour mixture. Stir well.

5   Scoop out ½ cup of the dough. Place it on the baking sheet. Press it into a 6-inch (15.2 cm) cookie.

6   Repeat step 5 with the rest of the dough.

7   Bake for 25 minutes or until they are light brown. Put the cookies on a cooling rack.

banana cookie bites

MAKES 36 COOKIES

INGREDIENTS

3 bananas

2½ cups old-fashioned oats

⅓ cup honey

1 cup dried apricots

⅓ cup applesauce

1 teaspoon vanilla extract

1 teaspoon ground cinnamon

½ teaspoon nutmeg

. . . .

TOOLS

mixing bowls

fork

measuring cups

measuring spoons

electric mixer

baking sheets

parchment paper

pot holders

spatula

cooling rack

1. Put the bananas in a large bowl. Mash them with a fork.

2. Add the oats, honey, apricots, applesauce, vanilla, cinnamon, and nutmeg. Mix with an electric mixer. Let the dough sit for 15 minutes.

3. Preheat the oven to 350 degrees. Cover the baking sheets with parchment paper.

4. Use a tablespoon to put the dough on the baking sheet.

5. Bake for 20 minutes or until they are light brown. Put the cookies on a cooling rack.

perfect
purple

COOKIES

MAKES 24 COOKIES

INGREDIENTS

1 medium beet, peeled and chopped

1 egg

½ cup raspberries

6 ounces vanilla yogurt

¾ cup whole wheat flour

1 teaspoon baking powder

1 cup flaked coconut

· · · · · · · · · · · · · · · ·

TOOLS

baking sheets

parchment paper

sharp knife

cutting board

measuring cups

measuring spoons

blender

mixing bowls

rubber spatula

pot holders

spatula

cooling rack

1 Preheat the oven to 350 degrees. Cover the baking sheets with parchment paper.

2 Put the beet, egg, and raspberries in a blender. **Blend** on low until the ingredients are mixed together. Add the yogurt. Blend on low.

3 Put the flour, baking powder, and ½ cup flaked coconut in a medium bowl. Stir well. Add the beet mixture to the flour mixture. Stir well. Refrigerate the dough for 20 minutes.

4 Put ½ cup flaked coconut in a small bowl.

5 Roll the dough into 1-inch (2.5 cm) balls. Coat each ball with flaked coconut. Put the balls on the baking sheet.

6 Bake for 10 minutes. Put the cookies on a cooling rack.

raspberry swirls

MAKES 12 COOKIES

Ingredients

½ cup butter
4 ounces cream cheese
1 teaspoon vanilla extract
1¼ cups all-purpose flour
¼ teaspoon salt
1 cup raspberry jam
⅓ cup chopped walnuts

Tools

measuring cups
measuring spoons
mixing bowls
electric mixer
plastic wrap
mixing spoon
rolling pin
spoon
baking sheets
parchment paper
sharp knife
pot holders
spatula
cooling rack

1   Put the butter and cream cheese together in a large bowl. Beat with an electric mixer. Mix in the vanilla, flour, and salt.

2   Lay out a sheet of plastic wrap. Put the dough on top. Press the dough into a flat rectangle. Wrap the dough in the plastic wrap. Refrigerate for 30 minutes.

3   Stir the jam and walnuts together in a small bowl.

4   Roll the dough into a 14-inch (36 cm) by 10-inch (25 cm) rectangle. Spread the jam mixture evenly on the dough.

5   Starting at a short end, roll the dough up tightly. Wrap it in plastic wrap. Freeze for 45 minutes.

6   Preheat the oven to 400 degrees. Cover the baking sheets with parchment paper. Cut the dough into 1-inch (2.5 cm) **slices**. Place the slices on the baking sheets. Bake for 15 minutes. Put the cookies on a cooling rack.

GLOSSARY

blend – to mix together so that you can't tell one ingredient from another.

container – something that other things can be put into.

counter – a level surface where food is made.

delicious – very pleasing to taste or smell.

layer – one thickness of something that may be over or under another thickness.

permission – when a person in charge says it is okay to do something.

recipe – instructions for making something.

slice – a thin piece cut from something.

towel – a cloth or paper used for cleaning or drying.

utensil – a tool used to prepare or eat food.